Kitchen
Music

Also by Lesley Harrison

Kitchen Music

Lesley
Harrison

Foreword by Kirsty Gunn

A New Directions Paperbook Original

Manufactured in the United States of America
First published as a New Directions Paperbook (NDP1564) in 2023

Library of Congress Control Number: 2023001746

10 9 8 7 6 5 4 3 2 1

New Directions Books are published for James Laughlin
by New Directions Publishing Corporation
80 Eighth Avenue, New York 10011

ndbooks.com

Contents

Foreword: The Sound of the Sea

A book of poems, a book of voices. A book that is also a map, an almanac, a report—of histories, of stories, of lands and waters. A book of poems made and arranged in such a way as to create harbors and enclosures: the contained order of narrative brought to a wild scattering of events; a careful arrangement of whale bones on a gallery floor to tell the tale of that great singing creature now stilled to silence. So does Lesley Harrison articulate vast ideas and weathers within the measured spaces of her stanzas and verses. She brings oceans inside her rooms, and catches the salt air of faraway places in the detailed work of fashioning these poems, each line and phrase flensed of all but the utterly necessary words that are spoken.

> between the houses, there is always wind

> as if the ground,
>   in its deep lurch upward
>   has trapped part of the air above the sea
>   (from "Hailuoto")

And who is it; who is speaking here?

> There is no weather in dreams. In dreams we move
> like fish in water, without resistance.
>   (from "Weather Reports You")

When I came to this collection first I was a reader, the printed words of *Kitchen Music* forming in the silence of my mind.

These were poems as though made out of others' texts, so it seemed—created out of archival documents, reorganized and reframed, or from fragments of a story, a past event witnessed or retold. But even then, when I was only reading, I also *heard* what I was reading. I could hear how each verse contained voices, speeches; here were folk tales being recalled and recounted, and songs, music: "Whale Songs," "Hymnal," "her song more a dream of music." I read the collection again and yes, how the forms indeed took shape as sets of notation, pentatonic in scale, reaching and keening. In "Rossie Moor":

> a field of young barley,
> the wind streaming
> white   green   white
>
> the wind, at sea in grass.

The infinitesimal care taken with the use of white space works as both stave and bar, treble and bass—even while the poem never quite settles to the traditional octave; it's as though it had never belonged there. Instead the poet leaves her cadences deliberately hanging, half loosened from the tonic note, arrested. Like the sound of the sea in a shell, or the note that can be heard in a high, fine wind. Here, from "Roses": "the door stands open, / the chilly bleat of seabirds / fills the open house"; or here, from "Hether Blether": "noon. / the sun absent, the island tranced in heat." So *Kitchen Music* has this quality, of silences and sounds all set in a very different kind of key to that with which we are familiar. "All day, the building sings to itself," Lesley Harrison writes in the long poem "Hailuoto," "in tectonic calm – A# and G – [. . .] octaves blooming over hours and / deforming / as light or wind declines." Again, the voice we're hearing is unsettled, tilted, restless. As though . . . as though . . . it does not belong.

And yet how this poetry does belong!

For I came at the collection a third time and now I was at my own kitchen table, with my daughter, and by then I was reading aloud. I was speaking out the words of this "Music" to the young woman who was listening with me, hearing . . . first one poem, then the next, the next. I began with the first line— "about 3 in the afternoon we got fast to a large fish"—from "Old Whaling Days," and we moved through "*grindehval*" in "C-E-T-A-C-E-A," "lying on a beach / wind blowing through its rotted sinews // unpitched / long, low tones / degraded by the air" to "emptied of herself, she floats / like an icon" in "Willibrord." And again, again: *Who is it; who is speaking here?* All at once the project of this book seemed to spring into life! Sound and tone and rhythm were caught up in one with meaning and sense and a charge of vitality, a force. . . . What was going on? My daughter and I asked each other that question, as the poems pulled us out of the kitchen and into their world. What was happening? As we felt ourselves vividly alive and lifted by an energy that was coming from—where? Like a wind or a tide these poems were tugging and drawing us onwards, so clearly and with such strength, away from where we were to a somewhere else. Then we knew. For Lesley Harrison has effected in this work of hers a mighty transformation. We could hear it. She had overturned a paradigm established for centuries and forced out of an old text a new poetics; the known and established histories about travel and seafaring adventures and the journey overwritten in a vivid, questing present tense of Harrison's own making: "the village has vanished." She has given a new voice—it sounded in our own speaking of these poems!—to the well-worn and memorized, the sea shanties and songs of lost children, the shipwreck tales and whale hunts; she had taken up the old white whale of the fixed and masculine narratives and made of its seas and weathers her own *Moby-Dick*, a female poetry

> in praises
> repeated, repeating
>
> one note
> falling like a flare
>
> again, and now again
> for hours
>
> the vast dark hung with
> ropes of song
>> (from "C-E-T-A-C-E-A")

No wonder these poems don't settle! To a base note. To an octave or tonic. Because Key Signature, Time Signature, Scale: What are these? Harrison has collapsed such preconceptions of order—the constituencies of a tradition, its music and narrative, along with their predefined ideas of beauty and the sublime and the transcendental and the metaphors and forms for these, the ballads and epics of the solitary traveller, of the unchartered ocean, the far horizon, the archival accounts of the chase, and the kill. She has written over them all in her own salt water ink, dissolving the bloodied stories of the past and turning their words into rich organic matter, shifting, uncertain, productive; the stuff of whale wombs and shape shifting and a presence that breathes and surges with life, revealing principles within the old texts that are instead generative in nature, matrixial and nurturing and elusive. From girl to woman to whale to water, Harrison shows us that it is female, the energy and presence that is inside those sea songs and stories we already know. "Wou as in Wound" becomes "E *as in dive*," based on John Cage's "Litany for a Whale"; the solo performance becomes a chorus we all sing. And those bones laid out mutely on a gallery floor? They speak, in a precise form of notation, not of a conquest but of the great animal herself.

—Kirsty Gunn
Sutherland, 2022

Kitchen
Music

Hoy, Orkney

The house, I remember, was built of wood and boasted three rooms—a dwelling-room, a cow's byre, and a store-room. Outside the building the angles were filled in with earth, which was covered with turf, the roof being similarly covered. The whole dwelling presented the appearance of a grass-grown mound.
—Captain T. F. Gellatly, *Adrift in the Arctic Sea*

Do not try to sing all the sections as a continuous musical thought. Rather, all the "ah's" form one musical line, the "eh's" another (melodically the most important), and the "huh's" a third. "Ah's" are always diffuse, "eh's" always bright, and "huh's" always pushing. Begin as if far away, gradually coming closer. . . .
—Emily Doolittle, *Social Sounds from Whales at Night*

Wou as in Wound

W = WOU AS IN WOULD   H = HU AS IN HUT   A = AH   L = LL AS IN WILL
E = E AS IN UNDER

—*Litany for the Whale,* by John Cage

WOU *as in wound*
HU *as in hunt*
AH *as in raft*
LL *as in fall*
E *as in breech*

WOU *as in bow*
HU *as in tump*
AH *as in slight*
LL *as in blink*
E *as in swell*

WOU *as in fluke*
HU *as in tongue*
AH *as in ebb*
LL *as in oil*
E *as in jaw*

WOU   *as in run*
HU   *as in calf*
AH   *as in eye*
LL   *as in blow*
E   *as in breath*

WOU   *as in sound*
HU   *as in hull*
AH   *as in wash*
LL   *as in shelve*
E   *as in dive*

Old Whaling Days

from the personal narrative of Captain William Barron, 1895

1.

about 3 in the afternoon we got fast to a large fish.
after a flourish
she succumbed to us.

2.

the sea began to increase, with showers of snow
as she was hastening towards the
outside of the fjord,

it was with difficulty
they could lash the fins together
and tow her to a place of shelter.

3.

the whale became furious
rolling over and over near us
when she struck the boat,

leaving some of her skin on the sheets.
the harpooner fired a bomb lance
which exploded in a vital part

4.
I saw her under water
she was beautifully distinct, and in slow motion
she lightly touched the vessel.
the concussion made her tremble

5.
one was struck –
she led us a nice dance
then went into the pack.

and during the whole time was
perfectly calm, the water smooth

6.
she came to the surface
and two more boats got fast,
leaving three to lance.

and in a few minutes
the sea, the boats and
the men were crimsoned

7.
to shew her rapidity, she immediately
rushed under the floe, down to the bottom

and was hauled up, having
broken her neck,
embedding in the dark blue mud.

8.
she was swimming on her side,
evidently watching our movements.
(but at too great a depth)

Weather Reports You

Vatnasafn / Library of Water, by Roni Horn, with interviews by Oddný Eir Ævarsdóttir. Stykkishómlur, Iceland

i.

My favourite weather is a north-easterly blizzard. This feeling is comfortable. I enjoy being in a breeze, or a drizzle out at sea. The weather is the sea.

ii.

A north-easterly is usually our best weather. It is bright and clear. The air is deep blue and fresh, like the good weather that follows a good catch, or a good wedding. Every moment is a new thing.

iii.

In summer, I get fed up with light. I feel full, over-satiated, like being in a closed room. The sky is empty. You have to move around. You have to be with other people.

iv.

The weather is part of my body. I shift my position in my chair according to the weather. I feel fine in calm, foggy weather. Then I can smell the sun. Talking about the weather is talking about oneself.

v.

There is no weather in dreams. In dreams we move like fish in water, without resistance. When we wake up, we are sluggish.

vi.

It is a wonderful time of year when the darkness is coming. It is when the sea starts moving. In August, when it gets dark at night, it is as if I am growing up further back in time. You feel that summer was a long time ago.

vii.

When it snows, the sky drops down to the village. This frightens me a little. After a storm, or a death at sea, the wind might drop and immediately it seems as if nothing had happened. Then grief is uncomfortable.

viii.

After a very cold Spring followed by a few good days, you fill up with a kind of joy. The world feels settled and empty.

ix.

The currents affect your dreams, as does the tide, and the moon.

x.

Weather is reflection and measure. Stories about the weather create false memories, conditioned by time, by a certain blindness. Our weather is always in the present. It is word-of-mouth.

Caa'in

"CAA'IN WHALES: the mode adopted for driving a shoal of these animals into shallow water to capture them."
—*An Etymological Glossary of the Shetland and Orkney Dialect*, 1866

"A Fortnight ago I & some of my people drove 23 whales onshore on this Island, & about 30 more have been got in the Bay of Firth."
—John Balfour, August 7, 1820. Balfour of Balfour and Trenabie Papers, Orkney Archives

upper **s c** apa   noswi **c** k

                    burra y   sc **a** pa bay
                    eda y   strons **a** y
                    cl **i** ffdale

       s **c** apa   bay of holland   f **i** rth
       sand **a** y
       st ol **a**   sa **n** day
          m **i** ll

bay   ba **c** kaskail
south ro **n**   lamb he **a** d
                                ed **a** y
          k erston   l **i** nklet bay
       scap **a**   **n** eebister

    ing **a** ness
                s **k** aill   s **c** apa
                sc **a** pa   backask **a** aill
                                  ing **a** ncɜɜ
                w **a** rebeth

          hu **i** p
                                c opinsay
          lop **n** ess   sc **a** pᴀ

                    knock**a**ll

                                s **c** apa bay
                                sh **a** pinsay

                                scap **a**

13

Convergence

[**resonance**]

my house holds sound
like the sea inside a shell:
a mundane music

of land wind – the flight forms of bare hills,
cleaving and adjusting,
thrumming against the walls

a sub sound of
lubbing rock pools, gulping
as the tide turns and boats hum in

or further out, to blinking turbines
with their on/off wave of air
a pressure in the head

a hush, an inaudible
hovering

[**sounding**]

a tremor, moving off
as continents adjust
in a dark, closed room

each sump, each crenellation
strung out from below in
tropical flarelight

puncturing the ocean floor, drilling or scouring
wailing or walling off
cul-de-sacs and closed doors, and

private, abyssal vaults
where vague forms sink or resurface,
rotting on beaches for hundreds of miles

[**displacement**]

tacet:
a held silence,
clear as porcelain;
a listening around

text interwoven
partly softly
as words hold the sound of all other words

out at the edge of earshot,
as eardrums respond to the sound of dreams.
　　　light the candle, he said.

[response]

Lewis fisherman Murdo Maclennan was interviewed for *Gaelic Psalm Singing in the Isle of Lewis* on *The Song House*, BBC World Service, presented by Ken Hyder.

as off the south banks of Scalpay,
far out, in crystalline darkness

on a quiet night, once the nets were cast
the sea still, the boats close together
we would go below deck, and praise god with a psalm

there was singing coming up through all the hatches
each boat each voice following on
singing beyond themselves

and the presence of everything around them
it gave you a heavenly feeling
as the hull inched slightly, and the tide held –

Hether Blether

An Orkney folktale, in which a girl goes missing from the island of Rousay and is found years later by her father on the mystical island of Hether Blether, west of Eynhallow.

i.
how, in the bright morning air
crossing the road with the world about her

the morning unusually still
and sunny, the islands laid flat below the cloud

she took the peat road up the hill
now right then left, now right, following a line

still rising, in a kind of dance, moving without hindrance
growing smaller and smaller

(the wind now cold,
the shore road blurring with sand, the sun clouding over)

there for a moment, then vanished.

haar –
the latent heat of seawater.

ii.
grinding up on a shallow beach
as the tide draws back, leaving them stranded:

lurching and heaving, sliding over kelps as they
lug the boat onto the turf, falling against its sides

now stretched and sprawling, the coarse grass hollow at their
backs
exhaling gasps of pollen, small dry heat

now shading their eyes against the glim as the
waves tilt mirrors at them,

the sea settling for a while
the sea sliding between rocks

as sweat slicks and cools down their backs,
their hands and necks slowly uncurling

as the tedium of hours of rowing
gradually falls away.

noon.
the sun absent, the island tranced in heat.

now sleep creeps over them,
Rousay now blue in the distance
the wind in abeyance, the wind abstracted.

there,
in the angle of a wall, singing the old lullabies:

her bowed neck, the fall of her hair
as she nurses her own child, latching him to her
in the nap of her shawl,

now putting him to sleep to watch him dream,
the privacy between them
deep and complete.

she motions them to silence, rocking him slowly with the
waves' rise and fall,
her song more a dream of music

almost inaudible, more thought than sung:
like wind through grass,
a quiet inside itself

or swans keening northwards
in high, clinking syllables,
trailing off in fine pale grey

now low and distant, full of sea longing
as somewhere near the tide turns
and four figures rise, and turn for home.

iii.
the story is told
of an island
invisible in rain or sunlight

at sunset,
a flake on the horizon

in winter, a silhouette –
like a boat, far out
weightless and emptied.

iv.
like waking to a dream:
soft dust sheets
billowing around them,

the surface brown black
their wake disappearing
in holes and curls

they lean and
pull forward,
rowing through hours of yellow light

and side-slip,
lurching as the
boat slews, correcting

finding the flaw in the current,
the sluggish
indrawing tide –

slow onset.

an amnesia,
a fugue state

v.

a wind-still morning;
the sea, an empty beach
where he is constantly arriving

the sun already high
the sea almost glittering

vi.
low skies bring rain in off the sea,
blackening the roofs of the town
where he sits in his single room

armchair, settle,
coal fire in the grate
its blue flame invisible

his window filled with cloud
like a hole to the sky.

the walls are white
like daylight in suspension.
this, the moment of her absence.

haar –
fragmentary moments of grief or heat

blow through, almost friable
like a sweep of snow

the boat stiffening and steadying as it
turns towards the dead

lights of the shore. in this new twilight,
the sea's plated surface bears weight

like a thought, like a cloud.
deep water shows as green patches.

vii.
a grief, held in abeyance:
the whole world
shapeless

in
paper white
mid-morning silence,

the old man
out beyond loss or mourning
locked in brightness

Kitchen Music

New York, 2017

> collage = REALITY
> —Joseph Cornell

i.
the morning after
with its "back to life" feeling.
manhattan breakfast:

a restaurant of
silver grey driftwood –
a feeling of water.

ii.
outside the coffee shop
a young bird alighted –
treethrushsong

iii.
a gulf of rain,
and the city sinks an inch.

at Penn Station, the lush tyres of yellow taxis –
umbrellas of Cherbourg
in the subway crush.

iv.
chance encounters:
old back yards,
reflections of the sun through curtains

from the sidewalk, gleaming
the city market,
"Hey Jude" among

bees and melons
a steel bridge, the Hudson
blank between the walls.

a corner bar.
a girl in a window.

v.
Thursday at the arboretum:
cool green
the café kitchen window open

and sounds tunnel in
– song sparrows,
butterflies that churr

vi.
downtown evening:
the sky towers of Manhattan
dark green against a stark aqua sky

then home, the sea
a new north blue.

the chill early March breezes
a wild piano music.
nostalgia wiped clear

vii.
this morning
among the tidewrack:
azimuth, whale bone

shoes and twine, a tedium of
cartons, floats
varia, et cetera.

a day owl, almost blue.

viii.
couch dream evening
entre chien et loup,
a high angelic sunset

"the earth with yellow pears
and wild with roses"

ix.
ephemera:
what minute (infinitesimal)
living can be

C-E-T-A-C-E-A

An exhibition by Marina Rees, using the bones of a long-finned pilot whale carcass recovered from Skjálfadi Bay. Húsavík Whale Museum, Iceland.

depot:
a beached whale

·

grindehval
lying on a beach
wind blowing through its rotted sinews

unpitched
long, low tones
degraded by the air.

the blue black silver of the fjord
in the meat of its spine,
its winglike arms almost blue.

•

how sound becomes colour:
wind over water
dark / light

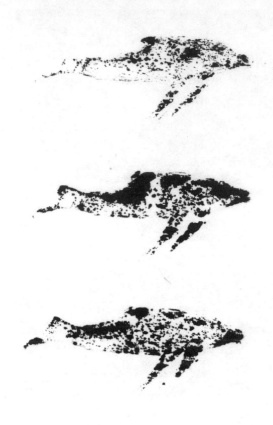

in praises
repeated, repeating

one note
falling like a flare

again, and now again
for hours

the vast dark hung with
ropes of song

.

sound substance:

minute adjustments of
pitch and ornament

the clicking patterns
rigid, discordant

the sternum
the cervical block

of lunar
knocks and hollows

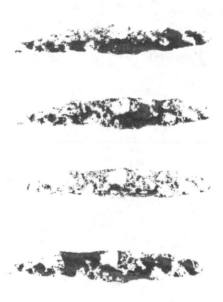

hvalreki:
("whale wrack") a windfall

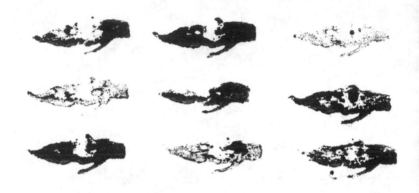

．

o cathedral:

like an aurora,
downsweeping

kindling the dark
with antiphons

the slow turn
of bulks in darkness

Roses

Embi: You said you had gone south to fetch your bride.

Pastor Jón: She was one of those phenomena . . . that has never been possible to explain except in the light of Jón Árnason's folktales.

Embi: English, Spanish, Irish?

Pastor Jón: Just from a croft down on the coast to the east. The parents of such girls send them away at confirmation age to earn their living as Cinderellas in the capital. Then suddenly it emerges that they are supernatural beings.

—Halldór Laxness, *Under the Glacier*

all afternoon,
the sound of grass
cyphery, frivolous

and leaves like bits of paper
whirled by the wind
in flurries of days and minutes

green and fallow brown.
summer into autumn.

i.
morning. the door stands open,
the chilly bleat of seabirds
fills the open house.

milkweeds blossom
in a stank of turf,
the cattle knee deep in yellow grass

the sun behind them.
clouds are motionless.

Old Jón   freed at last from practical desire,
       tending his cabbages
       as his world turns around him

       stirring in old flesh and fur
       and mouldery leaf clumps rotted down,
       their sweet ancient smell released

       and thrift, cudweed, wild thyme
       that bloom and falter on their own.

the horses   grown out of the ground,
       shoulder to shoulder
       tassled with moss and turd

       in medieval browns
       and faint gold leaf

       earthy, earthly
       almost constant
       sweating slightly from their journey.

ii.

time passes:
everyone aging in the moment that it

takes to turn the page now child now adult
now old man, rain-swept and serene

among these rank, warm creatures
with their soft tongue clicks and lipped hisses

rubbing and snorting round him,
his mouth forming words

as he slices the greasy yellow moss,
spooning in steaming rounds of shit and straw while

the mountains grind down
and the world goes past behind him.

Úa   fussing and flurrying –
unpacking her suitcase by the light of the single
bulb
(as the floor creaks and mutters)

appearing briefly, now here now there
now framed in the window,
lit like an angel in the cold, white glare.
later, sleeping

she fills the room like a deep sea mammal
sighing and turning
as the fire glows orange, then grey

or the glacier, remote as the moon
on the high plateau, its pale flanks sloping
steeply to the treeline, where small lights
are sometimes seen.

evening.
fog dissolves into dusk

and soon only white birds are visible
gliding without effort, like snowflakes
drifting in a calm

or falling asleep inside a book
the words merging into darkness
the white spaces gliding out.

iii.

a storm has emptied the ocean;
white veins riddle the mountain,
squalls of rain blowing over

as daylight arrives and arrives,
the old man feeding his horses
pacing the earth like a giant

as clouds condense
into dross and milt, and stone grey rivers.

Old Jón   when he saw her, he failed.

standing before him as if raised from the dead,
this warm earthy being
full flowered, staunch like a tree

leaning and steadying
as the wind curled and danced about her;

her own face worn and familiar,
the long ordinary years between them
shrinking in this winter afternoon.

she said his name, and said his name again.
he stumbled off, weeping with age.
she went inside and closed the door behind her.

Úa

undressing at the mirror
she sees herself full-length at last:

her spine pitched forward,
her sunburnt neck, the galls of her ankles

the open parts supple and yielding,
the whole rolling bladderwork

of breast, belly, shoulder
she'd learnt to be patient with, almost to placate.

her finger draws a line around her navel's
soft furrowing – a line of desire

that pulls her in around herself,
a world within a world

of love and weary longing,
blooming in darkness.

later, she lies as if asleep,
her tearless eyes
fixed on nothing.

iv.

how in the morning
there are still parts of twilight on the sea.

white in the blue-black
heaving ocean

the seabirds, serene in their homelessness.

Úa   driving into the distance, the tarmac hisses
           as the car speeds forward
           through miles and miles of soft grey rain

           a brief silhouette at the wheel
           as it flares past
           the old man hoeing the verge

           in pleasant day-to-day boredom
           and faint industrial fume,
           tending his peat mounds, and stanchions of
                                    old kale

           nursing the woody stumps.
           the small green mouthed orchid.
           the grass flowers, masculine and gentle.

Old Jón how once she had left, love began:
her form become abstract
the detail slowly eroding

the world resolving in her absence,
all times and seasons
shifting into place.

love – a reading backwards,
so all paths could
only lead to this.

watering the garden:
two streams
waver off one

way or
another
each finding

its own
way down

Iceland Poppy

Victoria Street, Kirkwall

it is snowing.

in the silence
of this bright space

a tight bud
creaking

prehistoric
as delicate as birch

dark white,
rooting.

Hailuoto

The island of Hailuoto first appeared in the waters of Gulf of Bothnia
in the first or second century AD. It continues to rise, and is now connected
to the landmass of Sweden at low tide.

.

not light not dark:

a blank north ocean
too far for birds

a catch on the horizon

.

chilled enlightenment –

of crushed grey green,
the sudden extrusion of a crest

a humboldt current drawing up the cold

the sea uneasy,
querulous and dense
the sea's slow upwelling

the sky an open eye

·

daylight, unworded:
like a film left to run on endless loop

the old sea bed brought up into the air
exhumed, exposed

the wind unrhymed, rough at the edges

the wind –
a song no music.

•

grass grows:
a faint effort, almost hum

as bays become lakes
lakes become swamps
swamps become meadows

blank brackish sponge
fastened to each other,
uterine and beading

eelpout, lugworm
fungal and beetle black
true wretches of the sea

•

at Marjaniemi

the pilot station
black against the sky,
its wooden ribs still sprung.

long strings are installed, tuned to its
resonant frequencies.

all day, the building sings to itself
in tectonic calm – A# and G –
a faint, tinny gamelan

octaves blooming over hours or
deforming
as light or wind declines,

like that part of the inner ear
whose thin hairs can detect a note,
even at great distance

•

between the houses, there is always wind

as if the ground,
        in its blind lurch upward
    has trapped part of the air above the sea

so that you round a corner into
        a local squall, still playing out
                                    still gasping

    like an old sea mammal,
    trapped on a sandbar   in cold daylight
                            outweighed by its bones

        now dull eyed and puckering

                            now slumped in sorrow

·

the white wind turbine, its helicopter shuddering as
if the news from somewhere else had suddenly
arrived without the pictures   and this was the sound today

of a flood in a suburb   an unseasonal avalanche   a
forgotten war in a small, hot country
a market   a mosque, gouged out   all limbs and bloody
                                                    bandages

•

fog
makes isolated gestures
like a hand without a body

•

landmarks are passed.
keeping near
offshore and losing

•

out of the visible
ahead,
a radio mast

•

fog, suspended.

an empty hallway
a tremor in a glass of water

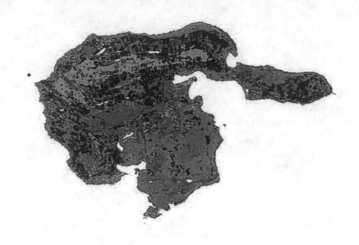

landstat.
a light clicks on and kills
the roar of light across the subpolar sky.

we have run aground
at the outskirts.
the rain from Oulu falls.

•

almost homelike:
an island sunk in darkness
in cobbled dry new forests

and the end of the street
is the limit of the world
where the ocean retreats and retreats

•

flute
in a tall tree, rehearsing

quotations
misplaced, part rhymes

reiterated,
lost in a world of lost

Oslo Water Colours
an exhibition by Callum Inness at the i8 gallery, Reykjavik

lamp black   /   titanium white

lamp black   /   titanium white

lamp black + yellow oxide   /   titanium white

blue violet   /   transparent yellow

sap green   /   perylene violet

quinacridone violet   /   may green

quinacridone violet   /   may green + yellow transparent

opera rose   /   transparent gold green

may green   /   perylene violet

olive green   /   magenta blue violet

mountain blue   /   transparent orange

anthracite lamp black   /   transparent orange

permanent rose   /   olive green + yellow transparent

anthracite lamp black   /   titanium white

lamp black   /   titanium white + neutral grey

Whale Songs

from *Harmonies of the World* by Johannes Kepler

                        here; consonance
            augmented   diminished

                    form
                            (as relying on
                                planetary move-
ments

    which thing these bulks

the longest, the middling

                    to
follow of themselves

                                    of
                                arcs
                                of
                                        single
                                following

                            , as
                another onc another
                    arcs

                              o
                           circle
                      narrower   :

              the two converging

           following distinct
)

                                              the smaller
                                              an octave,

        the last
          , irrational.

                a   true hymn
                            of bulls

            males,

                    bachelor

    begin to shadow
        imperfectly

                            1 : 3

                        2 : 5 and 4 : 5

            This kinship [*cognatio*]
    akin to   family

(intelligible, not audible)

a   singing
concentum]   in order

or passing

resolves by moving   downward

                                              too
                        or   near
                                      darkness

            dispers   unroll

                              each
                        angles at the

                                      clear above.

      black
          the sun shines
                        do four   encircle

forth clouds,
          showers

let   sparkle in its
   empty   and
here   breathes
                                              –

Willibrord

Willibrord (658–739 AD) was a Northumbrian missionary saint. It is recorded that, on the night of his conception, his mother dreamt that she swallowed the moon.

now clouding:

a whale in an abyss
– new, already old –
his soft heart bulging

his shell bones
the mishmash of his spine
his seahorse tail

all forming, soft as ivory
his bare head
occluded in a caul

stunned collision:
this dull heaviness that
pressed her back and down

frost feathering inside her, lining her womb
as the moon inched through and over
her petal white belly, her ribs

the nubs of her hips and spine,
wrapping her in white-black shrouds
now carved and hollowed

how real: this doll near her pillow,
perfect and remote
like the sun inside a cloud

all afternoon,
his still carved face
almost warm, breathing quietly.

a northern shoreline;
a concrete moon
a grey, concrete sky.

emptied of herself, she floats
like an icon
spreading hands, thighs

rimed with phosphorescence,
her breasts bound
her body blurring at the edges.

there is only joy
at this
slow ascension

salt numbing her birth wounds,
a bliss of cold water
bearing her up

Rune poems

The text commonly called the Icelandic rune-poem is only a poem by courtesy.

—R. I. Page, Viking Society for Northern Research, 1999

bulla   a talisman
        a genus of mollusc, with thin fragile shells
               of whales, the middle ear

fall   rain, blowing over
        the first sighting of a whale
        to become pregnant

blink   of cloud – a streak of lucid whiteness
        a trick, a stratagem
        to close the eye

sish   a crush between pans of ice
        a rimming and grinding
        a corpse (probably female)

tump   a tumulus
           a friction knot
           a tide lump, a varrel

tract   an anthem
           of birds, the contour feathers
           to haul or tow, to bore through

scart   a cormorant
           a cirrus cloud
           the mark of ink on paper

sound   a deep sleep, without dreams
           to touch the sea bed
           to strike or blow –

Rossie Moor

It is a fallacy to suppose that the music of the wild bird is
unprogressive . . . . The fact is, the bird has not arrived.
　　—F. Schuyler Mathews, *Field Book of Wild Birds and Their Music*

•

a field of young barley,
the wind streaming
white   green   white

the wind, at sea in grass.

　　　　　　　　　　　　teeick, teuchit, teeo, tee wup
　　　　　　　　　　　　　　lapwing

•

at Scurdie Ness
the lighthouse blinks at Denmark,
an old half-cousin.

3 p.m.
far out,
broadwinged birds
like angels, white in white.

[**Rossie**]

a clean sun
yellow, thinning to northern blue.

the geese, travelling in island groups:
            clanging, clamorous
        their frank exhalations
            and round brass syllables

        falling back to earth

[**seeps**]

arctic tern
    tirrick
    a liquid number
    a jarring of the tongue

                and six swans, arriving from Norway
                    like guests at wedding.

[the A92]

– tarrie bank – bog head – drunken dub – gelly loch –
  – inch ock – myre side – cauld cotts – silver wells –

[Binny Bank]
    a field full of windows

.

heron –
    old hebrew
    of the twitching grass
    of fat, gilling mud

[**the Sticks Burn**]

falls,

the cups and saucers of the burn
xylophonic

                                 – song sparrow
in the evening air.   in wood notes, grey gold
the cows wander, free as monks.

blackbird
        high
        on a thin tree

        a torculus
        of rippling spells

[**St Murdoc's chapel**]

·

a roundel
a sea door
a tree with a thought in it

·

the character of lichen
archaic, like aunts

clumped in off-white
antimacassar.

                 stonechat.
                   marks the air with empty brackets.

·

a yellowhammer
repeats, repeating

in dialects, in ancient forms of song

[the Mearns]

        twilight:
        blue, concentric
        like a snail in its shell.

february
    anechoic.
    a space too big for sound to carry.

Hymnal

Apis mellifera mellifera

[**Spring**]   thin undermusic:
aeolian, arousing
or whispery, thriving

now gossiping, their crowdy
knees and elbows,
all riddles and epiphanies

now off gallivanting
from their next-door front doors,
unlooping, climbing strings

humming their hums
as they fly to the sun and back

[**egg**]   brief iota –

a pip of wet
white something
moistened to the wall

now bend
now ripe
now swelling

now raised like an eyebrow

[**queen**]   fine faced and sleek
                our cleopatra,
                high in her eyrie

                a whore in a nunnery,
                paddling her bulk
                among oozy mattresses

                and wide saffron tapestries
                stitched with faint
                gold leaf

[**workers**]   and the godmothers:

                woody carmelites,
                performing their work-love
                in dark loft dormitories

                mumming and murmuring,
                nursing their godlings

                with old lullabies
                of operas and suicides
                and practical acts of love

[**inspection**]   look down!
at this hoi polloi,
on velvet gorse carpets

performing and performing their stories
now zithery, dispersing into corners

puzzling to disquiet like an
orchestra gone to pieces,
sending out doodlebugs

now riding out like valkyries
harrassing, hurling lightnings
piercing the smoke screen

like bees at bannockburn
clouding for battle, skirling their anthem –

[**June**]   rain, rain.

idling, we soloists
crooning our croons
in the half dusk, dreaming

a whitish plant of brownish blossom

while shuddery pearls of
water fall

[**pollen**]   what alchemists!
                 what jealous privateers, what
                 lapidary hoarders:

                 jewel pins of
                 tessellated amber, copper, coral red
                 tamped down, breaded to a pulp

                 packed like chandeliers and
                 stacked to the rafters

                 and old gold, slightly tarnished
                 forged into
                 wee thrupenny bits

[**starvation**]   like a nuclear winter:

                 a whole army, still assembled in ranks
                 stone dead in their bunker

                 gasless, grey as cement.

                 a private
                 hara kiri, a death pact.

[**supersedure**] old troglodyte:
old bauchle, old hebe
alone in her parlour,

singing to herself
this high summer evening,
bald as a husk and

twitching her curtains,
her kettle gone cold
her children off to Canada

Hansel and Gretel in Photos

In the beginning, or almost, for in the forest everything had always
already begun . . .

—Claudio Magris, *Microcosms*

a young wood
a curving flock of rooks
a low orange sun

[1]
it is as if we had all been astonished.
standing against a wall of trees
the sun remakes us as statues

light-struck, all surfaces and shadows.
this is what we remember to remember
and no one is growing any older

everyone alone in the daylight
as all photographs are real
and all stories are true.

but who is that, behind
slipping back into the forest,
and who is holding the camera?

[2]
now we are in the other room;
the two of them are talking in a corner
faces averted, deep in shade.

the light from the window cloaks them,
wool lined, elderly and private
their white hair gleaming

their backs rigid and bossed,
curved like wooden shields
worn smooth, facing outward.

[3]
this photograph was shot from below.
she poses, towering like a goddess.
the sky is bare, almost absent.
her blouse is emitting its own light.
a tree holds the clouds quite still.
his eyes are turned to the ground.
they stand by each other on the path
so close, they make each other tremble.

[4]
and now, here we are in the forest
high on a branch, looking down
like owls, folded and watchful;

and oak, and pollard, and rowan
and green elm, and damp, and woodworm
and two people almost in the frame

on another older, unmarked trail
that only they can follow.

where does the forest begin?
its entrances are invisible,
its paths both real and imagined

its deep breaths
neither heat nor melancholy;
just the feeling that this is.

[5]
our bedroom is curtained and airy.
our bedroom is empty, like a room
with pictures of woods and meadows.
the pictures reach deep into the wall.

the floor is turfed and familiar.
light comes and goes outside the window.
birds fly through the timbered walls
but we are not there to see it.

[6]
I am a sweet, fat baby
laced and ribboned
like an idol, placed in her lap.

her hands curl like tree roots.
she gazes, entranced
at the eighty years between us.

climbing trees, gaining distance.
the world, with its weight of nothing
leans and levels, leans and levels.

[7]
the village has vanished.
the air is pink and colder.
rooks clatter in the branches.

there is a sense of
something new amiss,
something whispery and nestish.

[8]
her house is sinking into the ground:
her sideboard is up to its knees
in china, and shortbread, and sweeties.
her old clock shows the time in years.

she waits on the sofa for us coming,
turning live coals in the grate
telling and retelling the future.
her eyes are blank as pebbles.

[9]
and now, here I am in my garden
gathering silences in jars
my house is as empty as water
my door is open to the air

and everything is perfect, undefined
and everything is yellow in the sun
and suddenly I'm older than they are
and now it is time to go home.

[10]
evening arrives in minutes:
the trees are hissing and sighing
leaves blowing through the rooms

the walls now soft and undecided
and ants tunnel under the paper
the pattern blurring and blinking

the text creeping into the picture
where everything is both false and true.

[11]
tonight all the houses are sleeping
the chimneys long towards the sky
our car is parked at the pavement
my hands are like moths on her face

she hides me up inside her hair
she is as comfortable as sleep
the street lamps humming in the dark
the forest is jagged and empty.

[12]
how in the end they simply went home,
returning at evening

walking backwards
through coarse grasses
and monstrous stumps of wood

gathering small discarded moons
which glowed, then
winked and died in their pockets.

fires burn the tops of trees
orange, orange, dull brown

the trees full-length against the sky
at sunset, as seen from below.

this is a picture of itself.
there are no shadows.

Notes

Old Whaling Days has appeared in *PN Review*. Part of **Rossie Moor** was published in *Antlers of Water: Writing on the Nature and Environment of Scotland*, ed. Kathleen Jamie (Canongate, 2020).

For **Kitchen Music**, imagery and quotes were gleaned from several sources including *Theater of the Mind: Selected Diaries, Letters and Files of Joseph Cornell*, ed. M.A. Caws (Thames & Hudson, 2000).

All of the images in **C-E-T-A-C-E-A** belong to the artist Marina Rees (www.marinarees.co.uk), to whom I am very grateful for permission to include them. Extracts from the poem appear in the film-poem *CETACEA*, with music composed and performed by Alex South (Royal Scottish Conservatoire) and Katherine Wren (RSNO).

In **Hailuoto**, the images of the emerging island were drawn from contour maps. The last image is from "Land Use Mapping with Landsat 5 TM Imagery: A Case Study from Hailuoto, Finland" by Alfred Colpaert (*Fennia* 171(1): 1–23, March 1993).

LESLEY HARRISON has published six collections of poetry, including the poetry pamphlet *Blue Pearl*, published by New Directions. She has lived and worked in Istanbul, West Africa, Mongolia, and the Orkney Islands, off Scotland's northern coastline. Harrison has held writing residencies in Iceland, Greenland, Svalbard, and The Center for Hellenic Studies at Harvard University. She lives in a small fishing village on the Angus coast of Scotland, where she also works as a teacher supporting language and literacy development.

KIRSTY GUNN is the author of several novels and collections of short stories, including the internationally award-winning novel about the Highlands of Scotland and the musical form of piobaireachd, *The Big Music*. She is Research Professor at the University of Dundee and Associate Member of Merton College, Oxford.